Around the county of NORTHAMPTONSHIRE
Clive Holmes
For Alex, Ellis and Lauren

Braunston Marina.

On a high ridge at the western edge of Northamptonshire, where the Oxford Canal and the Grand Union Canal meet, lies Braunston. On the south side of Church Road is a former windmill, built in 1800 for corn milling. It worked until 1890 and in the 1970s was converted into a private residence. Close by is the church of All Saints, its attractive spire being visible for many a mile. Down on the canal, Braunston Marina is one of the largest in the country. Most of the dock facilities, offices and warehouses are left from the late 1700s when Braunston was a large trans-shipment base. Today, boats of all shapes and sizes fill the marina and, viewed from beneath the graceful arch of the iron bridge at the entrance, make a quite spectacular sight. This elegant old footbridge from the 1830s, inscribed 'Horseley Ironworks' was salvaged from the Buckingham branch of the canal in 1962. In 1953 the Inland Waterways Cruising Company was formed at Braunston Marina, followed in 1956 by Blue Line Cruises, both companies providing canal boats for hire. Further development has made this area a base for the fitting, maintenance and repair work on canal boats.

© Clive Holmes, 2009
First published in the United Kingdom, 2009,
by Stenlake Publishing Ltd.
www.stenlake.co.uk
ISBN 9781840334432

The publishers regret that they cannot supply copies of any pictures featured in this book.

ACKNOWLEDGEMENT

Without the help of my wife, Kathleen, the research for this book would have been a lot less enjoyable. Together we extensively throughout Northamptonshire. I thank her not only for her support but also for her organisational skills and for her editorial ability.

BIBLIOGRAPHY

Arthur Mee, *The King's England. Northamptonshire*, Hodder & Stoughton, 1975.
J. Stigner, *Photographers Britain; Northamptonshire*, Alan Sutton, 1992.
Jack Gould, *Northamptonshire; Shire County Guide*, Shire Publications, 1988.
Northamptonshire Village Book, W.I. & Countryside Books, 1989.
T Noble, *Exploring Parish Churches in Northamptonshire*, Jema Publications, 1999.
T Noble, *Northamptonshire; A Portrait in Colour*, Dovecote Press, 1995.
E & L Renton, *Records of Guilsborough, Nortoft and Hollowell*, Beaty Hart Ltd. 1929.
Royal Northamptonshire, Northamptonshire Leisure & Libraries, 1989.
T Noble, *Exploring Northamptonshire*, Meridan Books, 1987.
Josephine Jerimiah, *The River Nene, A Pictorial History*, Phillimore & Co. Ltd, 2003.
R.L. Greenall, *A History of Northamptonshire*, Phillimore & Co. Ltd, 2000.
A Guide to the Industrial Heritage of Northamptonshire, Northamptonshire County Council, John Stanley Publishers, 2001.
Roy Mears, *Northamptonshire in a Nutshell,* Orman Publishing, 1995.
P Gordon Webb, *Portrait of Northamptonshire*, Robert Male, 1977.

The Packhorse Bridge, Charwelton.

Charwelton lies close to the Oxfordshire border, about four miles west of Daventry. In the Domesday Book it is recorded as Cearwellan, meaning 'well stream'. Centuries ago the infant River Cherwell rose in the cellar of the fine old farmhouse Cherwell Farm, close by the road to Hellidon but, following its demolition the river now rises in a pool close to a newer building of the same name. The river eventually flows through Oxfordshire joining the River Thames at Oxford. Unknown to many people, other than locals, is the fact that shortly after commencing its journey the Cherwell flows beneath the main road and under a 700 year old bridge as it leaves Charwelton. This notable old packhorse bridge looks tiny beside the modern A361 road, standing barely 4 feet high by about three feet wide. It has two pointed arches and is constructed of stout pieces of stone and gives a good indication of the period when transportation of goods was dependant on the strength of animals to carry heavy weights upon their backs and in panniers. This illustration shows the bridge and the War Memorial, unvelled in 1920, to commemorate the men of Charwelton and nearby Fawsley who fell in the Great War.

INTRODUCTION

Northamptonshire is not one of England's largest counties, but it certainly is one of the most attractive parts of middle England. With its villages of mellow stone houses, some with roofs of thatch and others roofed with the famous Collyweston slate, the architecture of the countryside presents a pretty sight. Add to this the numerous fine houses, the ancient churches and a history as rich, and full of intrigue, as anywhere in the land and Northamptonshire becomes 'a gem'. It can be likened to the Cotswolds, without the crowds, for here too generations have earned a living from agricultural farming, sheep farming and quarrying. Additionally in Northamptonshire boot and shoe manufacturing and iron smelting were developed.

With this rich and colourful background as my inspiration I was commissioned in 2004 by the Northamptonshire Chronicle & Echo newspaper to produce a series of pen and ink illustrations, together with text, for a series called 'Around the County'. Since then I have travelled the length and breadth of the county illustrating and writing of the places I have visited. Subjects of local, historical and architectural interest were included in this weekly series. This book is merely a small selection of illustrations and texts taken from the series, portraying 'Northamptonshire in Pen and Ink'.

New Street Oundle

The illustration shows the Post Office in New Street, Oundle, which opened in the early 1900s, with The Talbot Inn, built in 1552 with stone from the ruined Fotheringhay Castle and rebuilt in 1626, standing next to it. In the foreground is the war memorial which was unveiled on 14th November 1920. A water pump had previously stood on the site.

The town is famous for its public school, Oundle School, and for its many impressive buildings which form a fine backbone to this attractive market town. In its idyllic position on raised ground close by the water meadows of the River Nene the striking architecture of the town dates mainly from 17th and 18th centuries. It is worth taking a stroll around the town's centre in order to appreciate the quality of the buildings, one of the most imposing being Cobthorne House in West Street. This beautiful house was built in 1656 by William Boteler who was one of Cromwell's generals during the English Civil War. In 1944 it became the home of the headmaster of Oundle School.

The most northerly village in Northamptonshire, Easton on the Hill, stands close to the borders of Cambridgeshire, Rutland and Lincolnshire and has lovely views over the historic town of Stamford below. The illustration shows Church Street and the beautiful mix of stone buildings, some beneath Collyweston slate roofs while others retain their thatch. In the distance is the tall tower of All Saints Church with its 12th century origins. Inside the church is a tablet to the memory of Captain Lancelot Skinner who lost his life when La Lutine was wrecked on the Dutch coast in 1791. The ship's bell, The Lutine Bell, was saved and hangs at Lloyds of London. The gatepost of Skinner's fine house in West Street bears a tablet inscribed; *Captain Skinner RN of HMS Lutine lived here circa 1775 AD.*

Easton on the Hill.

A short distance from Captain Skinner's house is the "Priest's House". This much smaller building dates from about 1500 and served as the Rectory until a larger one was built in 1690. The original was used by visiting priests and as a school and during the following centuries served as stabling, housing for pigs and farm storage, until the first half of the 20th century. In 1967 it passed to the care of the National Trust.

On the left, the two storeyed building with dormers in the roof has a plaque on the front wall inscribed - W.B. 1830 - on it. Behind it are the converted stables of Easton House, which stands close by. This was the home of Neville Day, J.P. (1842–1925), an estate and land agent who managed a number of vast estates throughout middle England. In 1881 he arranged and financed the building of a reservoir and water was piped to taps in the village streets. He was also instrumental in the formation of the Eastern Gas and Coke Company in 1863, which supplied gas to the village at seven shillings and sixpence per 1000 cubic feet. In 1935, with the introduction of electricity, the company ceased production.

Sulgrave Manor

After the Dissolution of the Monasteries in 1539 Henry VIII had all their buildings and land sold. The Manor of Sulgrave, belonging to the priory of St. Andrew at Northampton, was sold to Lawrence Washington who built the fine house we know as Sulgrave Manor about 1560 and for 120 years it was home to his descendants. John Washington, an army colonel and the great great grandson of Lawrence Washington, sailed to the New World in 1656 and settled at Mount Vernon in Virginia. George Washington, the first president of the United States of America, was the great grandson of John Washington. The American flag, the Stars and Stripes, is said to have derived from the Washington family's coat of arms of three stars above two bars.

In 1914 the house was refurbished and presented by a body of British subscribers to both the people of Great Britain and the United States of America as an acknowledgement of the 100 years of peace between the two nations. In recent years a visitor centre has been opened to cope with the many visitors from all over the globe.

The tanning of hides was a well established trade in Earls Barton by the 13th century and would continue until 1984. The footwear industry continues yet at the Barker factory which was opened in 1987 by the late Queen Mother.

The church of All Saints dominates the village from its high vantage point, the magnificent 80 feet high Saxon tower is regarded as one of the finest in England. Built in A.D. 970 the tower has no buttresses but pilaster strips, thin pieces of stone projecting slightly from the surrounding surface which from a distance give the appearance of timber frame construction. The nave was built during the 1100s by the Earl of Northampton, Simon de Senlis.

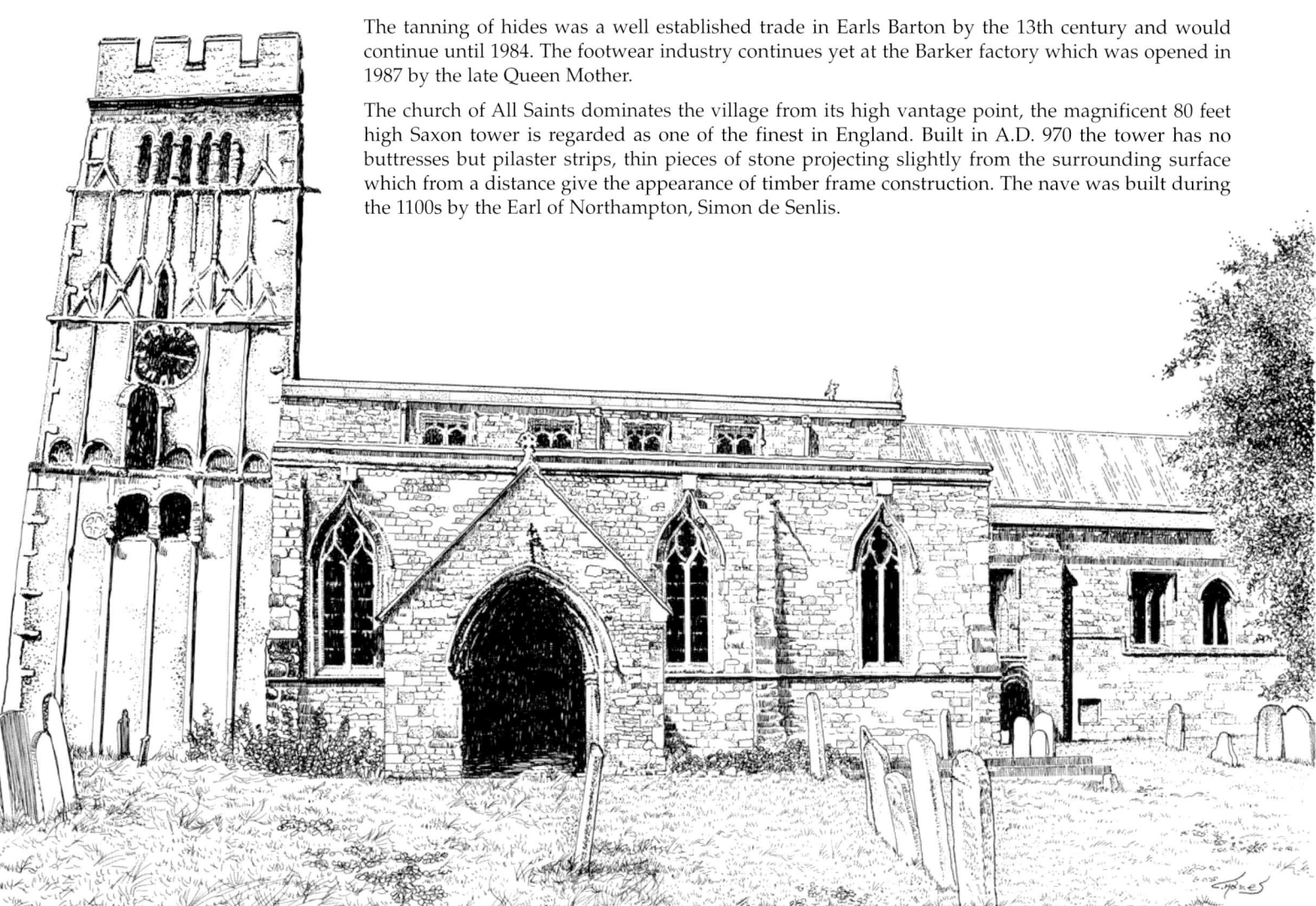

All Saints Church, Earls Barton.

The Medieval bridge spanning the river Nene at Thrapston.

Since granted its weekly market by King John in 1205, Thrapston, on the River Nene, has grown and expanded with much of its development taking place in Victorian times. Now known as Cedar House, and used by Thrapston and District Council, the stone built Union Workhouse was put up in 1836 at a cost of £4,000. The Magistrates Court, built in 1860, later became the Court House Hotel. During the 1800s Thrapston had two railway stations, Bridge Street Station and Midland Railway Station, both of which closed between 1964 and 1972. Stretches of the former line between Northampton and Peterborough are pleasant walking routes beside the River Nene and the lakes left by gravel extraction.

It is still an attractive town and has retained many of its old attractive buildings. The river has always played a part in Thrapston's life, but to facilitate a road link with Islip, a bridge was constructed around 1663. In 1795, however, a great 'sea flood' swept in and destroyed five of its 24 arches. It was rebuilt by the end of the 18th century - much as we see it today, probably one of the most attractive bridges in the county, amidst the trees and wetlands of the Nene. Many years ago a toll had to be paid to cross the bridge; those excluded were 'those going to church or soldiers'.

St Mary's Church and the Old School House, Orlingbury.

While the leaves on trees add beauty to our landscape they frequently obscure it. So it is at Orlingbury, for like so many village scenes it appears quite different during the winter months. This view of St. Mary's Church and the picturesque old school house of 1845 cannot be seen together during the summer months owing to the tree in the foreground. This is the village centre, the almost triangular village green, clustered around which are a variety of attractive old houses together with more recent dwellings.

Dominating the green, and the surrounding countryside, is the tall square tower of St. Mary's Church. Below the belfry windows are bands of carving and from its battlements four tall pinnacles reach skywards. Richard Hussey, a Birmingham architect, rebuilt the church in the early Victorian Gothic revival style in 1842-43 and placed an attractive rose window in its chancel.

The last wolf in England is said to have been killed in the 14th century by Jack of Batsaddle who lies in the sanctuary, sculptured in alabaster, a warrior in chain-mail on his 14th century tomb. The Chymbale or Chybnalles family were Lords of the Manor here during the 17th century and are well represented in the church. A brass plaque in the nave names eight village men who died in action during World War I.

At the tender age of 15 years Thomas Tresham became the head of one of the most powerful families in the county and he had inherited one of the largest estates. It seemed that his intention was to connect the Old Bield of Lyveden via beautiful gardens and woodland with this new summer house or lodge. Standing a couple of miles from Brigstock the 'new Bield', or building, appears today almost ghost-like as an eerie silhouette of Sir Thomas Tresham's fixation with religious shape and symbolism. A fervent Roman Catholic he suffered imprisonment as a consequence of his beliefs and his son's implication in the Gunpowder Plot.

Built in the shape of a cross it has large, bold, five-sided and five feet long windows and constitutes a fine example of Tresham's understanding of architecture. Work started in 1594 but by 1605, when he died, the project was still incomplete. The build quality was of the highest standard and that it has stood without a roof and windowless for four hundred years is testament to this. With its elaborately sculptured inscriptions on its sides and bands of blank shields which are interpreted by the National Trust Guide Book as starting from the north face of the north wing, as follows: - 'Jesus the Salvation of the World. Rejoice, O Mary Virgin-mother. But the word of his Cross is even foolishness to those perishing. Jesus, blessed is the womb that bare thee Mary, Virgin unwedded spouse God blessed thee for ever, O Mary God forbid that I should glory save in the Cross of our Lord Christ.' The Passion of Christ and the five wounds are commemorated in the external decorations. The house and grounds are today in the care of the National Trust and during recent years much has been done to restore them to their former glory.

Shown here is Braybrooke's ancient bridge straddling the River Jordan; with the three storey brick built Bridge House, and the church of All Saints, beyond.

The bridge carries the road to Desborough, about three miles to the east, and an inscription tells us it was built by Sir Thomas Latymer of Braybrooke Castle who died in 1401 - the work was completed the following year by his wife. Alas, all that remains of his castle are mounds and traces of a moat. Sir Thomas was a Crusader and inside the church, is an oak carving of Sir Thomas holding a shield on his left arm.

All Saints Church dates from the 13th and 14th centuries, with a 15th century tower with gargoyles below its graceful spire. High in the tower is an old doorway which led to a rood loft. The Griffin family succeeded the Latymers at the castle and a monument to them in the church, dated around 1570, includes depictions of the griffin of legend. The square font, with its fine detail of snakes and a mermaid eating fish, is an example of Norman craftsmanship.

The River Jordan bridge, Braybrooke.

All Saints' Church, Northampton.

The Saxons arrived in Northampton around A.D. 650, followed by the Vikings and, later, the Normans. During the Great Fire of 1675, like many other buildings in the town, the Norman church of All Saints was so badly damaged that it had to be rebuilt.

Today the church dominates the town centre. and is considered to be one of the finest examples of church architecture of its period outside London. It mainly dates from the 17th century for little else, except the crypt below the chancel and the base of one of the earlier church towers, survived the flames. Many important civic ceremonies are held at All Saints and in the side aisle is the gilded seat for the Mayor, dating from 1680.

Charles II donated 1000 tons of timber from the Royal Forest of Whittlewood to help rebuild the town after the fire, and to mark this kindness, an annual procession used to be held in the town; nowadays, a wreath of oak leaves is placed on his statue in the church on Oak Apple Day.

Just off Gold Street, in the centre of Northampton, the narrow, Kingswell Street runs beside the Grand Hotel and here is one of the town's old gems. With gold letters on a background of deep wine coloured tiles is the title BECKETT AND SARGEANT'S SCHOOL ENDOWED ANNO DOMINI 1735. It is a narrow building from front to back built of red and black bricks with an elaborate combination of pale coloured stone and ironstone decoration around its windows. The design is repeated around the front door, above which, is the charming stone figure of a young girl. This presumably represents a pupil of the school during the 18th century, as she wears a tall crowned cap tied under the chin, her skirt is clear of her ankles and she appears to be carrying a piece of needlework.

Mrs Beckett, the widow of a surgeon in Cheshire who died in 1719, took up residence in Northampton with an unmarried sister, Miss Sargeant. The ladies were comfortably off, owning a great deal of property in the town, and in the autumn of 1735 drew up a trust deed enabling them to use the rents from some of their properties to finance a school for 30 poor girls. It is not clear if this is the site of the original school but it is known that religious education, needlework and house craft formed the backbone of the syllabus. In recent years this eye catching old building has become the home of a Youth Advice Centre.

Beckett and Sergeant School, Northampton.

The Welsh House, Northampton.

The only building in Northampton's town centre to survive the Great Fire of 1675 was the Welsh House on Market Square - now beside the entrance to the Grosvenor Shopping Centre. Built in 1595 by Dr. Prytherch, from the Isle of Anglesey in North Wales, on a site he purchased for £80. The illustration shows it following its restoration in 1975. A plaque on the wall tells us that the name, Welsh House, derives from the motto, 'HEB DYW HEB DYM DYW A DIGON' placed above the main window by Dr. Prytherch in honour of his Welsh heritage and translates as 'Without God nothing, with God plenty'.

The Eleanor Cross, Hardingstone.

King Edward I was so devastated by the death of his wife in 1290, for theirs it seems was a true romance, that he erected an elaborate cross at each of the thirteen places that the funeral procession stopped overnight at on its journey from Harby in Nottinghamshire to Westminster Abbey. (Of the three of the crosses which remain today, at Waltham Cross in Hertfordshire, Geddington and Hardingstone in Northamptonshire, the Geddington cross is the most intact.)

This impressive, slender monument at Hardingstone was an outstanding example of medieval craftsmanship before being eroded over the centuries by the weather. It was carved from Helmdone stone in 1294 by John de Bello and the four beautiful statues within the monument were carved by William of Ireland. The monument stands atop a flight of nine stone steps and unfortunately has lost its top.

A little way to the south of the centre of Northampton and still standing in the grounds of what is today parkland the abbey of 'de la pre' was one of only two Cluniac nunneries in the country. Founded in 1145, by either Simon de Senlis or possibly by his son, the Cluniac nunnery of Delapre was the place to which the body of Queen Eleanor was brought. All night the abbess and the nuns watched and prayed beside the coffin. The following day the long procession continued its journey with the King riding behind her coffin. It is said that Edward I wrote, 'Living I loved her tenderly, and I shall never cease to love her dead.' Throughout its lifetime it has witnessed a number of events which were important in the history of England.

Due to the importance of Northampton during the 15th century, the armies of Henry VI and the Earl of Warwick faced each other on the water meadows between the River Nene and the Nunnery of Delapre. Rumour spread that the Bishop of London and the Archbishop of Canterbury had also arrived in order to try to mediate between the two opposing sides. Alas, there was to be no compromise and in 1460 the Earl of Warwick's armies overthrew the armies of King Henry VI. He was captured and together with other prisoners spent the night of the 10th July at Delapre. Unfortunately the Battle of Northampton was only one of many battles fought during the War of the Roses and the conflict between the Houses of Lancaster and York continued until 1487.

Following the Dissolution of the Monasteries the building was converted to a fine house during the 16th century and altered considerably during the 19th century by the Bouverie family who owned the house from 1764 until 1946 when Northampton Corporation acquired the whole complex, together with 586 acres of parkland, for £56,000. By 1954 the Town Council wanted to knock it down, but it was saved and became the home of the County Records Office until 1992.

Little remains of the original building today, most of the existing structure dating from about 1750. The stable block, not visible in my illustration, was built between 1750 -1765 and was renovated by John Goff, the County Architect, in 1971.

Delapre Abbey, Northampton.

This small terrace of four delightful old cottages has faced out onto the tiny green at Dallington since 1673 when they were built to accommodate two old women and two old men. The inscription on the building reads 'Let none dare to violate them' and 'Vengeance is God's'. They were built by Richard Raynsford who was a supporter of Charles I, and for this support he was made a judge and became Sir Richard Raynsford. The Raynsfords sold their estate to Sir Joseph Jekyll who, in 1720, built Dallington Hall on it but as Sir Joseph had no children the estate passed to the Spencer family who were the ancestors of the late Princess Diana of Wales.

Within sight of the almshouses is the medieval church with the pinnacle tower constructed during the 14th century. Inside the church are reminders of the Arts and Crafts movement of the early 1900s. A window, dedicated to the memory of Margaret, Viscountess Althorpe who was a member of the Spencer family, was produced by William Morris in 1906 as was the tapestry behind the altar.

The Manor House, Ashby St Ledgers. The Plotting Room is shown inset, top right.

In Northamptonshire we have many lovely villages but Ashby St. Ledgers is stunning. Ascebi, as it was called at the time of Domesday, has a 14th century village church dedicated to the Blessed Virgin Mary and St Leodegarius. It has wall paintings from A.D.1320 to A.D.1500 and a font that is Norman in origin.

Close by is the old manor house which dates from Elizabethan times, having been built by one of the Catesby family. As manor houses go this is a large one but much of the enlargement was designed by Sir Edwin Lutyens during the last century. It is still, however, beautiful. Privately owned, this magnificent building is not open to the public, but the front of the building can be seen from the road.

Near the church is the entrance to the old manor house. (inset) This old stone gateway with its timber frame upper storey, is said to be the place where the Gunpowder Plot was planned and has consequentially become known as the plotters room. Robert Catesy was a Roman Catholic, and had been imprisoned and fined for his religious beliefs became one of the leaders of the Gunpowder Plot of 1605. Upon discovery he was shot while trying to escape.

The Victorian Primary School and Elm Cottage, Milton Malsor.

At Milton Malsor village centre a triangular shaped green is overlooked by modern houses and a terrace of cottages converted from the former malt house of a local brewery. The village store is tucked away at one corner of the green and a short distance away, up Green Street, is the delightful old Victorian primary school across the road from which is Elm Cottage with its thatched roof.

Down Collingtree Road is the former village bakery, which was still functioning until the mid 1960s, and opposite, Rectory Cottage is thought to have been the residence of the rectors of Collingtree, a local village, in the 16th and 17th centuries. Throughout the village there are numerous attractive stone cottages dating from the 17th and 18th centuries.

Holy Cross church has a 14th century battlemented tower with a short crocketed spire set on an octagonal base, but the church is best known for its windows. At the end of the south aisle is a beautiful 'wheel' window with stone carvings of great detail. In the north arcade are the church's oldest parts, the stout circular pillars which date from the late 12th century. The church possesses a large cup shaped font with a 12th – 13th century base, while in the south chapel a former priest's doorway has been blocked up.

The Welland Viaduct, Harringworth.

In 1879, belching steam and smoke, the first passenger train crossed this remarkable feat of civil engineering as it spanned the Welland Valley. It was constructed between 1877 and 1879 for the Midland Railway Company by the London contractors Lucas and Aird in order to provide a much needed link between Kettering and Oakham. My illustration shows this magnificent structure at Harringworth before it crosses the River Welland and enters the county of Rutland.

The Welland Viaduct, also known as the Harringworth Viaduct, must have rated as one of the wonders of its time when it was completed. It stretches for almost a mile across the Welland Valley and is visible from much of the surrounding countryside. It consists of 82 arches, each having a span of 40 feet with an average rail height of 57 feet. 71 of its 81 piers measure six feet in thickness, the remaining ten being twelve feet thick and the whole structure being made from around 30 million bricks.

The railways of this country were built by a large force of rough, tough, hard drinking and hard working labourers. They were known as navvies who travelled from all parts of the country seeking work where physical strength and stamina was in great demand and where there was little need for education. They would arrive on site in ones or twos, or in gangs often with their own bedrolls, picks and shovels. Understandably they were treated with suspicion by local villagers for they were men with no permanent home. They went where the work was and often there was friction between them and those who resided locally.

My illustration shows the old mill beside the River Nene at Wadenhoe. A water mill has stood on the same site here certainly since the 12th century and possibly even since Saxon times. The present building was extensively refurbished during the 19th century before finishing its working life and being converted into a private house in 1972.

Away from the river, beyond the mill, lies the delightful village of Wadenhoe. One of the most attractive small villages in the county with a fine mixture of buildings dating back for centuries.

In Church Street Nene Cottage dates from the 18th century while next door, number 33, is a century older. Almost

Wadenhoe Mill.

opposite, The King's Head was constructed before the English Civil War and was extended two centuries ago. Facing it are numbers 31 and 32 converted from four terraced houses to two during the last 200 years. Formerly a village shop, number 28 dates from the 17th century, while Caroline Cottage, built in 1839 as the village school, closed its door to pupils in 1955.

In Main Street is the post office. George Ward Hunt was the Chancellor of the Exchequer in 1868 and was for a time First Lord of the Admiralty. During 1871 he had the tiny post office equipped with one of the earliest telegraph systems in order to keep in touch with London. His family resided at Wadenhoe House which is said to date from 1657. He became famous for forgetting to take along his red dispatch box on Budget Day and that is why today the Chancellor traditionally holds up the dispatch box before travelling to the House of Commons.

The church is a short distance away from the village, perched high up above the river. The tower is of 12th century saddleback design, one of the few to

Victoria Mills, Irchester.

Fronting onto the River Nene just to the north of Little Irchester are the Victoria Mills. This purposeful looking building was built in 1866 and greatly enlarged during the last century. Until 1969 grain was transported here by narrowboat. Whitworth Bros. Ltd. still mill flour here today, but the boats using these stretches of the upper Nene are now mainly pleasure craft with the occasional working boat still plying its trade.

To the south of the mills, between the river and Wollaston Lodge, and to the north of Irchester, close to the 17th century Chester House, Roman remains have been unearthed. Whilst the name Chester denotes its Roman connections it is generally thought that the name Irchester is derived from the Anglo-Saxon name of Iren Ceastre meaning iron fortress. 400 Saxon graves were discovered in 1873 during excavations for ironstone. This was a major industry here until 1941 and provided regular work for the village residents. Since the workings closed much tree planting has taken place and in 1971 the Irchester Country Park was established on the site.

The Church of Saint Mary and All Saints, Fotheringhay.

In 1370 Edward Langley, the fifth son of Edward III and founder of the powerful House of York, commenced work on a college and a castle at Fotheringhay and after his death his son, Edward of York, continued the work. The college was founded in 1411. Together with the castle, in its commanding position beside the River Nene, must have made a magnificent vista from the surrounding marshland.

Mary, Queen of Scots was imprisoned in the castle in September 1586 and beheaded in the great hall on 8th February 1587. It is said that Queen Elizabeth I referred to Fotheringhay as 'that terrible place'. Rumour has it that the executioner stayed the night at Castle Farm.

Although today little remains of the castle, the church is still very much in evidence in spite of being much smaller than in its heyday because of the destruction of the college and the church in 1548 following the Dissolution of the Monasteries. It is a superb example of perpendicular architecture and is surmounted by a fine lantern tower. Inside, beside the altar, are memorials to Edward, Duke of York who died at Agincourt in 1415 and to Richard Plantagenet who died at the battle of Wakefield in 1460 and whose son, Richard III, was born at Fotheringhay Castle in 1452.

My illustration shows the elegant arched bridge stretching across the Willow Brook with the old gate house dated 1878 on the right at tiny Blatherwycke. The bridge carries two dates 1656 and 1726 together with a plaque with the initials of the O'Brian family, who were the Earls of Stafford, entwined in the Stafford Knot, for the fine Elizabethan Hall which once stood amidst beautiful grounds was built by Sir Humphrey Stafford. Alas nothing remains of the Hall today as it was so badly knocked about when used by the army during the Second World War that it was sold for £1,500 in 1947. It was purchased by a builder who then had it blown up and used the resultant building materials for construction purposes elsewhere. At that time such materials were in short supply.

On the north side of the bridge are the large man-made Blatherwycke Lakes which cover about 54 acres. With the removal of the Hall most of the surrounding land, previously part of the gardens which encompassed the Hall, is now used for farming and the only connection with the history of the former residents here is in the church. The ancient church, now in the care of the English Heritage, is dedicated to the Holy Trinity and stands on a steep bank to the west of the Willow Brook. Although the tower is Norman the church is mainly known for its contents rather than its architectural significance. Inside the church is the famous tablet to the poet Thomas Randolph who died whilst staying with the Staffords in 1635. It begins thus:-

'Here sleepe thirteene together in one tombe
And all these greate yet quarrele not for room.'

The bridge at Blatherwycke.

The old Grammar School, Guilsborough.

At Guilsborough beside the main street and facing the 'Ward Arm' public house, itself a fine building, is the former grammar school a superb example of Jacobean architecture in pale Northamptonshire stone, dating from 1668 when it provided education for about 50 local boys until 1909. Above the entrance porch is a sundial of 1821 with the inscription 'Fronte capillata post hoc occasio calva' which means 'opportunity must be taken by the forelock'. The school was built by John Langham who was a local man, born about 1584, who made his fortune trading as a turkey merchant and grocer in London. In 1972 the school was converted into private dwellings.

The village church, dedicated to St. Etheldreda, has a tower and spire of 13th century origin but the whole building was extensively refurbished in 1613. The Art and Craft movement is well represented here with a number of memorial windows in the chancel which were designed by William Morris and Sir Edward Burne-Jones for Adelaide, Countess Spencer, who died in 1877. The village has a colourful past as it is a very ancient one. It had a Roman encampment close by and there is evidence of a Saxon settlement before Domesday. In 1612 two local women were hanged for witchcraft and before the battle of Naseby in 1645 General Fairfax and his troops camped here.

About five miles west of Towcester, within a maze of minor roads, is the attractive village of Blakesley cum Woodend. The Woodend part of its full title comes from times long since past when it stood within the forest of Whittlebury. The Hall at one time a hospice of the Knights of St. John of Jerusalem stood there, until 1957, when it was knocked down. The last Lord of the Manor at Blakesley was Charles Bartholomew who died in 1919. He was a benefactor to the village and something of an innovator. In 1903 he had a narrow-gauge railway laid from the hall to the nearby main line railway station. His train of open carriages was hauled by a pair of steam engines which were imported from the U.S.A. In 1909 the famous Northampton company of Bassett-Lowke provided a petrol driven locomotive with the grand title 'Blacolvesley' to add to the rolling stock. During the early days of the Second World War the whole system was dismantled and transported to Yorkshire. Bassett-Lowke became one of the most important industrial model-making companies in England, producing scale models for shipping companies in addition to locomotives and rolling stock. They also manufactured small numbers of high quality model railways.

My illustration shows the view down Church Street with its mixture of fine stone buildings. Further down to the left is the medieval church of the Virgin Mary, almost completely constructed of ironstone. Possibly the most remarkable monument inside the church is a brass wall mounted portrait of Matthew Swetenham who died in 1416 and had been the bearer of the bow to Henry IV. Close to the church the oak tree was known as Dryden's Oak, after John Dryden, the poet, who resided at Blakesley before settling in London. He was born in the north of the county at Aldwinkle in 1631 before moving south where he later aspired to the title of Poet Laureate.

Church Street, Blakesly cum Woodend.

Southwick lies in a slight valley amidst green hedgerows and tall trees. To the north of the village and on a slight slope is the forest of Rockingham and at the edge of the village is one of the most interesting of this county's historic small houses.

Southwick Hall, built in the 14th century, has been modified and updated during each century until recent times; it is a delightful conglomeration of fine gables and tall chimneys. Still privately owned, Southwick Hall is open to the public at certain times of the year and is a 'must' for those interested in the history of this part of Northamptonshire. Within the building there remains a medieval chapel with windows depicting the various lords of the manor dating back to 1351. The main part of the house is Elizabethan.

Over the centuries the Hall has been home to three families. The Knyvetts, resided here during the 12th century, in an earlier building, until the mid 1400s. John Knyvett was a judge, the second layman to become Chancellor of England and an executor of the will of Edward III. The estate was then bought by the Lynnes whose family lived here until the 19th century when it was bought by the Capron family, formerly of Stoke Doyle.

The very name of Naseby stands out in importance when compared with most other villages in England. It is fitting indeed that it stands high in middle England for here rise the rivers Avon, Severn and Nene. A stone column was erected in 1936 to commemorate the battle in 1645 and also to correct the error of the older memorial which was built in the wrong place in 1823 on the site of an old windmill beside the road to Market Harborough.

The battle was fought about a mile away from the village and was the last chance that Charles I had to maintain his hold over the English people. Victory at Naseby would have cleared the way to London for the King and Prince Rupert, but that was not to be. During May 1645 the King had sacked Leicester and proceeded to Oxford, later retreating to Market Harborough pursued by the New Model Army of the Parliamentarians. After seizing the initiative against a much stronger force, the Royalists were defeated by the skill of Cromwell's cavalry. 5000 prisoners were taken and imprisoned in Northampton's churches. Following this defeat the King's cause was never to recover and a year later he was placed under house arrest at Holdenby House.

Today the village and the surrounding areas are quiet, almost sleepy and there is little to show of what took place here. The Church of All Saints has in its north aisle a ten foot long table, said to have been used for Cromwell's meal after the battle and for the Royalists before the battle. The table came originally from Shuckborough House which was formerly the local inn. Shuckborough House was partially pulled down in 1773 but the rest still remains in its much altered state as Shuckborough Farm. The church itself has both Saxon and Norman connections but in the main dates from between 1200 to 1500A.D.

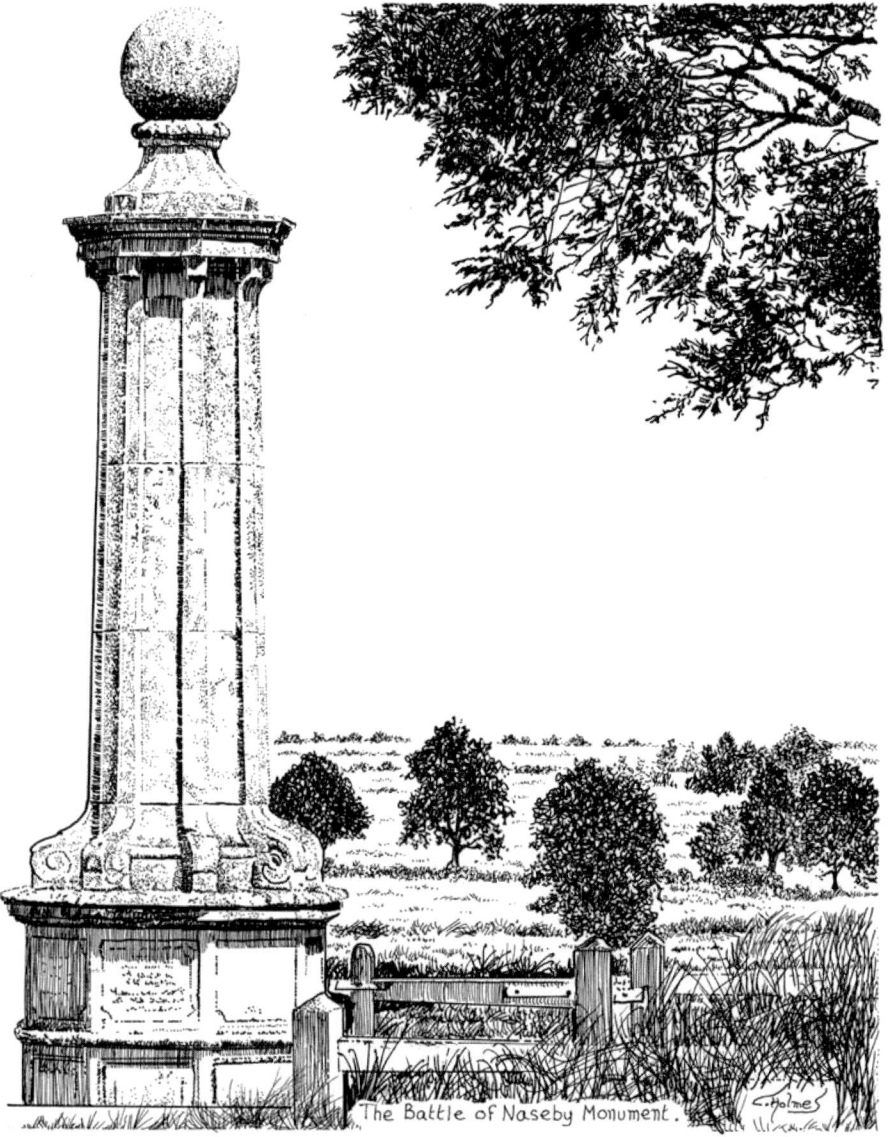

The Battle of Naseby Monument.

At the time of the Domesday survey the village was known as Asbi but at sometime after the Norman Conquest the Lord of the Manor was Robert de Meres and over the years the two names combined to become Mears Ashby.

The 12th century church of All Saints stands on high ground looking down from its fine vantage point above the old stone dwellings grouped around it. Seen from Ladys Lane, Nunnery Cottage with a thatched roof, is shown on the left of my illustration and is dated 1779, whilst just beyond, number 29 has a carved head in its gable and is white with a slate roof. Beyond is the short, square battlemented tower of the church. Above the triple arches of the belfry, the tower has rows of corbels on each side with a short pinnacle at each corner of the battlements. Inside the church, above the chancel arch, is a large 'Doom Painting' which was restored in 1984. Just inside the Norman south doorway is the octagonal font, also Norman in origin. In the south aisle is a 'Wheel Cross', possibly of Viking craftsmanship. Occasionally these have been found in the north of England but rarely this far south.

A local tale of a ghost in the church graveyard tells of a woman who, in August 1785, was accused of witchcraft. She was duly dunked into the nearby fish ponds and drowned. The unfortunate result of this trial, it seemed, was to prove her innocence and as a result it was said that she returns to haunt each August.

The old water mill, Duddington.

Duddington is a delightful conservation village, a few miles south of Easton on the Hill and just off the A43 road, beside the River Welland and adjacent to the county of Rutland. The viewpoint I have chosen for my illustration is from the bridge, medieval in origin, which spans the River Welland. It shows the former water mill built by Nicholas Jackson in 1664 with its mansard roofs. The mill is now used as business premises. The village is indeed a picturesque one with many of the buildings having Collyweston slate roofs. At the village centre is the much restored manor house dating from 1633 an impressive building behind wrought iron gates.

It is generally assumed that due to the ground sloping away toward the river on the west the tower was constructed on the south side of St. Mary's Church. Set at a corner of the chancel, on its Norman base, a short spire was added during the 13th century. The church porch is a most impressive piece of 14th century architecture. It still retains the original roof beams and has a massive timber door with heavy hinges and robust ironwork. In the nave are six arches which date from Norman times, two of which at the east end of the north arcade carry a strong zigzag design. The chancel, while still standing on older foundations was largely rebuilt in 1844.

Sudborough.

The village of Sudborough lies close by the Harpers Brook just off the busy A6116 to the north of Thrapston. Centuries ago this was part of the vast forests of Rockingham and even today the surrounding areas are well clothed in woodland and copse. The main street has a gradual curve and runs almost parallel to the Harpers Brook and, as my illustration shows, contains some very attractive terraced cottages, with the village pub, The Vane Arms, on the far right. Further down the street the dwellings are of mixed ages, some with tile and others with slate roofs. This is indeed an old village for there is evidence locally of ancient earthworks and fish ponds of an early monastery.

The church of All Saints is just beyond the main street. It is small and certainly enhances the appeal of the village. The building was mainly constructed during the 13th and 14th centuries with much refurbishment being completed during the 19th century. In the north wall of the chancel is the crossed legged figure representing Sir Robert de Vere. He was the standard bearer to the son of the Earl of Salisbury who led a Crusade to the Holy Land in 1249. His legs are crossed as an indication that he died fighting in the Crusades.

This illustration shows the buildings of the former mill at Blisworth situated beside the Grand Union Canal which reached Blisworth in 1796 at which time it was called the Grand Junction Canal. Just beyond is the much widened and strengthened bridge No. 51 which carries the Towcester Road into the village centre.

Blisworth was a main coaching centre on the Stratford and Cheltenham routes and the old coaching inn, the Grafton Arms, was one of the main hostelries in the vicinity. In the mid 1800s it was converted into a desirable private residence. The greatest development of the village took place during the period of Britain's 'Canal Mania' when canals were constructed throughout the land. The position of Blisworth, close to the centre of England and within almost touching distance of the manufacturing heart of the Midlands, meant that it was well placed to expand as the canal became busy.

The Grand Union Canal, Blisworth.

Blisworth Hill gave the engineers a problem. It was decided that a tunnel should be built and, during the construction period, the Blisworth Hill Railway was built to transport the off-loaded cargoes over the hill in order that they could continue their canal journeys. The railway ran for five years, being opened in 1800. The Blisworth Tunnel, opened in 1805, is the longest navigable canal tunnel in the land at 3075 yds. It was, at that time, a fantastic feat of engineering skill.

Ancient Britons, Romans, Saxons and Normans have all contributed over the centuries to the development of the town of Towcester. 'Lactodorum' was the name the Romans gave to their settlement here on Watling Street. Later, during the invasions by the Danes, Edward the Elder, son of Alfred the Great, instigated the fortification of the town. During the English Civil War it was said to be the only Royalist town in the county and during the days of coach travel it became an important stop between London and Holyhead. The Talbot Inn, constructed in the early 1700s became a famous coaching inn and later it housed a bank.

Another early 18th century coaching inn, The Saracen's Head, is famous from the 'Pickwick Papers' by Charles Dickens who is said to have included Towcester in the form of 'Eatanswell' in the novel.

At the corner of the old Market Square is the former town hall, constructed in 1865 and now used as an office. Close by is the old Chantry House. Founded in 1448 by Archdeacon Sponne it is surrounded by high stone walls with an entrance through a stout stone arch. To the right of the Chantry House is Chantry Lane with the church of St. Lawrence ahead and cottages to the right. Two carved pillars of a Norman doorway have been incorporated into the fabric of the chancel arch of the church and the remains of a Roman hypocaust and floor tiles have been unearthed in the south aisle.

The church is thought to have been built originally by the Saxons in A.D.920, but with its Norman contributions, for the most part dates from the medieval period. A bright and interesting building the church reflects much of the work done for the town by William Sponne, a great benefactor to the town who established the Grammar School in 1440 and was the rector until his death in 1448.

The church of St. Lawrence and adjacent cottages, Chantry Lane, Towcester.

My illustration of Ravensthorpe shows the picturesque old post office in the High Street. Built in 1610 with walls of mud beneath a thatched roof it was extended on the far side in 1875 in order to provide accommodation for the postmaster and his family. Beyond the post office are two handsome stone houses, the nearest one has a corrugated iron roof and beneath that tall crop of ivy, to the left of the illustration, is a telegraph pole almost completely hidden from view.

The village is large with a number of sturdy old stone buildings as well as many houses constructed during the last century. In 1982 the village held a Wool Festival in an effort to raise funds for local amenities, the main event being an attempt to make a replica of the well-known Throckmorton coat of 1811. The idea was to duplicate the conditions of sheep-shearing, spinning, washing and drying the cloth and cutting and sewing up the coat. The original coat had been produced from start to finish in 13 hours and 20 minutes but this one was completed in 12 minutes less than the original time. Today the coat is housed at Althorp House.

The oldest building in the village is the ironstone church of St. Denys, known to earlier generations as the church of St. Dionysius. Constructed during the 13th and 14th centuries it is a simple building and all the more attractive because of this. The tower is perhaps the most eye-catching part of the building with its archway leading into the nave, the three arches on each side of which complement it. The small chancel is modern by comparison and dates from the 19th century. The pulpit is Jacobean and is dated 23rd April 1619 (St. George's Day). The font, with its crude carving of a horse, is Norman in origin and the suit of armour, which

Kettering.

This illustration shows one of the finest buildings in Kettering and one of the few remaining from the 1700s. A fine example of the architecture of the period it is symmetrical about its centre, having three sets of windows on two storeys to the left and right of the main doorway, above which, on the upper storey, is the seventh window. In the roof are three small dormer windows which are surmounted in the roof by three groups of handsome chimneys.

Standing proudly on Lower Street, it is known as the Carey Mission House and was the meeting place for those keen to form the Baptist Missionary Society. Here William Carey, a resident of nearby Moulton, rose from his humble beginnings as a shoemaker to be one of the county's most famous sons. In 1792 he and Andrew Fuller founded World Missions. It is said that at the meetings subscriptions were collected in Fuller's snuff box, a humble start to the world's first missionary box. Thomas Gotch, 1748-1806, lived opposite in Chesham House built in 1762. In addition to financing William Carey he was instrumental in the founding of the leather and footwear industry in Kettering in 1778.

The Bell Inn, on Bell Hill, Finedon.

This is one of Finedon's best known landmarks, the handsome mock-gothic structure, the Bell Inn. It stands on Bell Hill on the site of an old inn, of the same name, built in 1598. This former hostelry was demolished about 1830. In 1873 the unusual mock-gothic façade was added and, for reasons unknown, the date of the accession to the throne of Edward the Confessor, 1042, was added. At the same time a statue of his wife Queen Edith, who owned the manor at Finedon before the Battle of Hastings, was placed in an alcove at the front of the building.

This illustration shows the church St. Mary the Virgin at Titchmarsh, with its 15th century tower. It stands 99 feet high from its base to the top of its weathercock and seven bands of carvings run around it. Eight carved pinnacles reach up from its parapet; it is a tower fit for a cathedral with its sundial and clock. On the south porch and dating from the days before the clock was invented are ancient scratch dials. Scratch dials were the earliest form of sundials and divided the working day into 'tides' rather than hours e.g. noontide, or the times of the day which related to specific religious services.

Inside the priest's doorway chevron carvings are present on its Norman archway, whilst on the outside the Early English builders have given the archway a point. Most of this superb building dates from the 13th and 14th centuries, while the chancel arch, with its crowned head of Henry VII, dates from the 15th century. Thatched stone cottages face the church on the curved main street and former farm buildings and old village business premises have now been converted into fine homes.

Holdenby House.

Holdenby House was claimed to be the largest house in 16th century England. Built by Sir Christopher Hatton, Lord Chancellor and favourite of Elizabeth I in 1607 it was bought by James I. In 1647 it became the 'prison' for four months for his son Charles I. During the Civil War the house was used as the Royalist headquarters and therefore the king was no stranger to the building and to the grounds. Part of the garden is still called the 'King's Walk'. In early June 1647 Cornet Joyce, with his troop of Parliamentarian cavalry, came to collect the king and take him into the custody of the Army since the king had lost the Battle of Naseby in 1645.

After the execution of Charles I the house was sold in 1650 to a Parliamentarian, Adam Baynes. Following the sale he had it demolished with the exception of the Elizabethan gateways of the outer courtyard, to this day still displaying the date 1583, and the kitchen wing. This wing formed the basis for the rebuilding of the house between the years of 1873 to 1875, smaller than the original but still quite magnificent.

Kirby Hall.

Kirby Hall was designed by John Thorpe for Sir Humphrey Stafford of Blatherwick and a note by the architect on the original plan,'Kerby where of I layd ye first stone A.D.1570' confirms the commencement of the building work. It was one of the finest examples of architecture of its time in this part of England and was completed in 1575. On the death of Sir Humphrey the house was sold to Sir Christopher Hatton and eventually the estate descended to the son of a cousin who was created Baron Hatton of Kirby in 1643. During this period Inigo Jones was employed to remodel the north front. He also replaced stone mullion windows with large wooden ones and added a central attic, amongst much other work.

From this time little was altered at Kirby and this beautiful grey stone building stood amidst its fine gardens, almost isolated. By the early years of the 19th century England was under threat of invasion by Napoleon and Kirby Hall was selected, not least because of its isolated situation, as a suitable dwelling for King George III and Court should the occasion demand. The threat gradually subsided and in spite of being most suitable for occupancy by Royalty it was deserted by the 1820s. Its owners, the Finch-Hatton's, had other fine residences and Kirby Hall was left to fall into ruin. Today the house and grounds are cared for by English Heritage.

Clipston, The Old Grammar School.

Situated about five miles south of Market Harborough and a few miles west of Naseby Field, Clipston is a large village with a number of fine houses. One such building, 'Prince Rupert's Cottage', situated on the gently sloping High Street reminds us of the close proximity of Naseby and that final battle of the English Civil War in 1645.

A little further up on the left hand side of the High Street is the dignified looking brown stone building shown in my illustration. It has three storeys beneath a high pitched roof and three gables with stone mullioned windows protruding from the front of the building. Today this fine old structure houses the village primary school. It originates from the endowment and building of a 'grammar' school by Sir George Buswell in 1667. He was heir to his parents' lands and a man of huge wealth who was the High Sheriff of the county from 1662 to 1663. He died aged 41 years in 1667. A monument in the church stresses his benevolence, piety and exemplary life. Boys living in six local parishes were taught at the school for free. The schoolmaster had to be single and a graduate of either Oxford or Cambridge and a member of the Church of England. The original building was designed by a local resident, Matthew Cole. The school was restored in 1927. Mr. Blackwell of Kettering was the architect responsible for the refurbishment and reorganisation of the school which was officially reopened by the Bishop of Peterborough on January 4th 1928.

Easton Maudit.

To the right of the church porch, of St. Peter and St. Paul at Easton Maudit, in my illustration is a young tree, beyond which is a huge elm tree stump measuring over 20 feet in circumference. John Bunyan preached beneath the elm between 1653 and 1658. John Wesley also preached here from 1740 onwards. The cottage to the left is the former school house and dates from the mid 19th century. It is built of limestone and has a pantiled roof while the thatched building beyond it is the Well House also built of limestone but dating from the 17th century. The village takes its name from the Mauduit family who became its owners in 1131.

The Reverend Thomas Percy became the vicar of St. Peter and St. Paul at Easton Maudit, in 1753, at the age of 24. A brass plaque on a pew in the church tells us that Dr. S. Johnson, O. Goldsmith and D. Garrick worshipped here with other members of the Garrick Club during the time that the Rev. Percy was the vicar, he too was a member of the club. In 1765 he published a collection of ancient ballads. One of the finest English poets of his time he was noted for his anthologies. His proposal in verse to Anne Guthridge was described by Robert Burns as the finest ballad in the language.

The courtyard, Apethorp Hall.

Claimed by some to be one of the finest amalgams of all time, Apethorpe Hall houses some of the most magnificent Jacobean rooms in England. Almost forgotten amidst the countryside of north Northamptonshire this great house had been bypassed and neglected until English Heritage came to its rescue. It was constructed during the late 1400s with many additions made by later generations. The Constable of Fotheringhay Castle, Sir Guy Wolston, was the original builder but about 1551 the house was acquired by Sir Walter Mildmay who, in readiness for the visit of Elizabeth I in 1566, created a state suite in the South Range. James I visited on eleven occasions during his reign of 1603 -1625, whilst Charles I also visited between 1625 -1649, to enjoy the sport of the great forests of Rockingham. During the years of 1622 to 1624 the state rooms were remodelled and the Long Gallery was constructed. The Orangery dates from 1718. In the mid 19th century a first floor conservatory was added and loggias in the east range were remodelled.

In 1617 the 1st Earl of Westmorland inherited Apethorpe Hall, through marriage. It remained in the hands of the Earls of Westmorland until the 13th Earl sold it in 1904 to Mr. Leonard Brassey (later Baron Brassey of Apethorpe) whose grandfather had amassed a fortune from building railways. In 1949 Lord Brassey sold the house and it became an approved school. When closed in 1982, it became the property of English Heritage. At the time of writing English Heritage are seeking a resident who will have sufficient funds to further refurbish this magnificent old house.

Ye Golden Lion, Wellingborough.

This lovely old building in Sheep Street, known as 'Ye Golden Lion', Wellingbourgh, was constructed as a house in 1540 and it displays a fine combination of limestone and ironstone lines and, as can be seen from my illustration, a stout timber- framed bay projects from the left side of the main entrance. During the 17th century it became the home of Thomas Roane, a yeoman farmer, who modified and refurbished the house and in 1830 it became an inn. It stands with handsome stone buildings beside it and the elegant Swanspool House, of 1778, close by. In 1320 the abbot of Crowland Abbey started a swan farm in this area, hence the name Swanspool. The house and the gardens were given to the town in 1918 by Mr. F.C. Chamberlain, the house now being used as an administrative centre and the gardens as public parkland.

Wellingborough was founded by a Saxon leader by the name of Waendel and for about 600 years the place was known as Waendelburg or Welingburgh. The town is situated on a hill adjacent to rich ironstone beds and close to the junction of the rivers Ise and Nene. Iron foundries, tanneries and flour mills provided work for the residents of Wellingborough for centuries and made many families rich. If we delve back into history we find that Wellingborough was granted to Croyland Abbey in Lincolnshire by King Eadred in A.D.948 and continued under their ownership until the Dissolution of the Monasteries in 1539.

Only a few miles to the west of Kettering is the small village of Thorpe Malsor, almost hidden in woodland and accessed by a series of narrow, undulating lanes. On Church Way stands the church of All Saints, to the left of which and slightly behind it is Thorpe Malsor Hall. The church dates from the 13th and 14th centuries but was much restored in 1877 by Clapton Rolfe. The Maunsells, who resided for generations at the Hall, were generous benefactors to the village. Robert Maunsell, served as a midshipman under Lord Nelson on H.M.S. Maidstone in 1804 later becoming captain of the 91 gun H.M.S. Rodney. He ultimately received the K.C.B. and was appointed a Commissioner of Greenwich Hospital.

From the time of the English Civil War comes a very touching story from this village when one of the members of the Maunsell family lay badly wounded on the battlefield at Naseby. As he was about to be removed for burial a young woman, who happened to be the daughter of an apothecary, turned up and felt his pulse. She pronounced that he was still alive and due to the soft skin of his hands she could tell that he was a gentleman. The story tells of her removing her petticoat and wrapping the man in it. Eventually he recovered from his wounds and rewarded her with a position as his housekeeper, she received an annuity after his death.

Thorpe Malsor Hall and church of All Saints.

Main Street, Colleyweston.

Situated in the north of the county and close to the Rutland border Collyweston is well known for the production of stone roofing slates from thin sheets of limestone. Between the layers quarried here a natural 'sap' becomes enclosed, which tends to freeze in winter weather thereby aiding the 'slicing' process. For 500 years or so the men of Collyweston produced this reliable roofing material until the industry ceased production in 1967.

The old High Street is lined with charming old stone houses. My illustration shows the view at the bottom right hand side where the 'Corner House' and the "Steward's House", centre, are bathed in winter sunshine. The Steward's House was built around 1620 and has this name on the original deeds. The house was once a grocers shop. The Corner House was originally an inn and was also used as the village post office between 1963 and 1977.

In the village there are a number of modern houses but stone buildings, hundreds of years old, are numerous. Of course most of them have slate roofs and the village hostelry on the Main Road is aptly named 'The Collyweston Slater'.

Cotterstock.

Originally a Roman settlement before the Norman Conquest, Cotterstock had always been referred to as 'a place where people gathered'. At the time of Domesday 'copper-stoc' was recorded as its correct title. Many centuries later there were two manors at Cotterstock one of which was connected to John Gifford who was Canon of York and founded a college of priests consisting of a provost and 12 chaplains at Cotterstock in 1338. He later became clerk to Queen Isabella, wife of Edward II, and later still was to serve Edward III in a similar position. The manor, consisting of a couple of mills along the River Nene, a fishery and a considerable acreage of the Forest of Rockingham, was granted to the college by Queen Isabella. The second manor was known as Holts and was inherited by a John Norton or Norden, a parliamentarian, who in 1656-8 had the present Cotterstock Hall built. Here an attic room was given over to John Dryden, the poet, and it was there that he wrote many of his fables.

The village church at Cotterstock is dedicated to St. Andrew. Architecturally it is something of a mixture of different periods, the chancel being the only major part still existing from the time of John Gifford. The herringbone carvings in the church are said to be of Saxon origin and the west doorway, beneath the modern statue of St. Andrew, was built by the Normans. In 1420 Robert Wintringham, who was Canon of Lincoln, died and a fine brass portrait depicts him in his robe of office. My illustration shows the bridge, rebuilt in 1956, to accommodate the heavy vehicles, crossing the River Nene, to and from the mill. To the left is the former Victorian mill which was damaged by fire in 1968 and since being refurbished has become a private dwelling. At the centre is Mill Cottage whilst to the right is the Mill House, an attractive three storeyed house built for James Rickett who owned the mill.

Middleton Cheney is a large village lying about six miles west of Brackley and consists of a pleasant mixture of old stone cottages, former farm buildings and considerable recent development.

My illustration shows the attractive dwellings in Church Lane and the church of All Saints, beyond, with its acutely sloping porch roof. The porch is said to be one of only three in the county to have such a roof, the others being at Corby and Chacombe.

Back in 1086, the time of the Domesday Book, the Norman Lords of the Manor of Middleton were the Chenduit family. Over the years the name evolved into Cheney, hence Middleton Cheney. Much later in May 1643, one of the earliest battles of the English Civil War was fought close by on what is now the site of a housing estate. It was a Royalist victory which, under the command of the Earl of Northampton, killed 217 Parliamentarian troops and took 300 prisoners; 46 of the Parliamentarian dead were buried in the churchyard of All Saints. Dating from the 14th century the church has a spire 150 feet high. The pre-Raphaelite stained glass windows are considered to be amongst the finest examples of the work of William Morris and Edward Burne-Jones.

Church Lane, Middleton Cheney.

Down the High Street, Preston Capes.

The delightful old village of Preston Capes, about six miles south of Daventry, sits on a ridge almost 600ft. above sea level. The village derives its name from Hugh de Capes who was lord of the manor after the Norman Conquest of England, and at one time his castle stood close to where the manor house stands today. Just to the west of the church of St. Peter and St. Paul the land drops away quite steeply and from here, in good weather, fine views across the Nene Valley may be enjoyed. Also visible from this vantage point are the ancient Iron Age camps of Borough Hill and Arbury Hill. Long before the church was built a Preaching Cross was erected here at the point where worshipers gathered. Today the head of the cross is visible on the outside of the church in the east wall of the south aisle. The battlemented tower dates from the 15th century but the nave arcade is older having been constructed about 1200A.D., while the grotesque corbels in the chancel are said to be Saxon fertility symbols. The bench ends are rich with tracery, one with a coat of arms and others with poppy heads and given that the church was much restored in 1858 all seems to blend in well, the old with the more recent work.

About a quarter of a century after the Battle of Hastings a priory was founded here and the 16th century rectory close by the church is said to occupy the same site. Nearby is the former village school, constructed in 1845. It was enlarged in 1871 but closed in 1965 and was used more recently as a private book room. My illustration shows the attractive view down the High Street to the edge of the village. Unlike the rest of the buildings in Preston Capes the Archway Cottages were built during the first half of the 18th century as four dwellings for workers at the nearby Fawsley Hall. The cottages have a connecting archway built of red brick and are described by some as being 'castle like'.

Brigstock, Hall Hill and the Market Cross.

My illustration shows the centre of the village of Brigstock, Hall Hill and the ancient Market Cross which was erected after Elizabeth I had passed through the village during her reign. As early as 1466 Edward IV granted the right for weekly markets to be held at Hall Hill. Just to the south of Hall Hill, down the aptly named Church Street, is the Church of St. Andrew dating in part from the late 800s. It has a rare stair turret at the base of the main tower and together with the great arch, which leads through from the tower to the nave, is the oldest part of the existing building. Badly damaged by the invading Danes in the late 9th century the church was restored and additions made spasmodically from Norman times until 1873 when major restoration was carried out. Above the south door is a room where in past times the priest resided.

The Manor House is to the west of the church beside Harpers Brook. The oldest part of the Manor House is its Great Hall which dates from around 1150, the house being a former royal hunting lodge. It was also used on 27th February 1207 by King John for his court. Rumour has it that his ill-fated journey to the Wash, where he lost the Crown Jewels, started here. West of the Manor House is the former mill recorded in the Domesday Book of 1086 when the village was known as Kings Brigstoc. Brigstock was, however, an Anglo Saxon name meaning 'Birch Tree Stump'. Just over a mile from the village is the 'Bocase Stone', which stands about three feet high at Harry's Park Wood. Its two inscriptions indicate that at or near the stone stood the 'Bocase Tree', One local theory says (the place where men came to practice archery).